TOOLS OF THE BELIEVER

Danielle,
You are
Blessed
Inspiration
to all!
Love you,
C. Lor

Daniele,

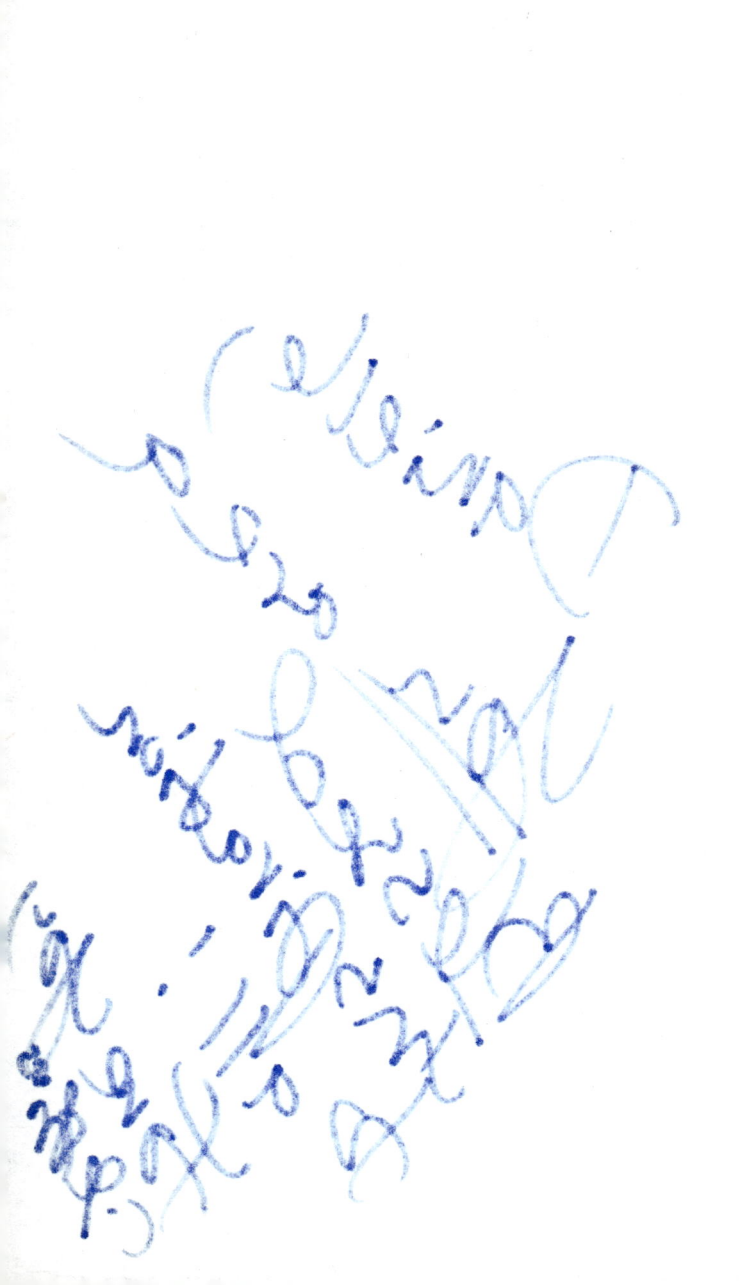

Jou are a
fantastic
Organizer!!
Thanks.
Cheers,

TOOLS OF THE BELIEVER

CHECKMATE: ACCESS DENIED!

by Cheryl Jeffries

 **Tools of the Believer** is committed to excellence in the publishing industry.

The company reflects the philosophy established by the founder, *Write the Vision, Rightly Dividing the Word of Truth,* based on Habbakkuk 2:2, "And the LORD answered me, and said, Write the vision, and make it plain upon tables, that he may run that readeth it."

If you would like further information, please contact us:
1.366.577.4711 | www.toolsofthebeliever.com
Tools of the Believer | P.O. Box 20851, Winston-Salem, North Carolina 27120 USA

Tools of the Believer: Checkmate: Access Denied!
Copyright © 2010 by Cheryl Jeffries. All rights reserved.

No part of this publication may be reproduced, stored in a retrieval system or transmitted in any way by any means, electronic, mechanical, photocopy, recording or otherwise without the prior permission of the author except as provided by USA copyright law.

All scripture quotations are taken from the Holy Bible, King James Version, Cambridge, 1769.

Book design copyright © 2010 by Tools of the Believer. All rights reserved.

Logo design by Kevin Gibson

Published in the United States of America
ISBN: 978-0-9834195-0-1

Dedication

This book is dedicated to my mother,

Eleanor Jeanette Lewis Gibson,

for a lifetime of

love, support, and encouragement.

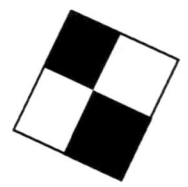

Acknowledgement

My LORD and Savior, Jesus Christ – in Him
I live, and move, and have my being

Rufus Christopher Jeffries, my Boaz – for
supporting the vision God has given me

The children that the Lord has lent to me for a
season –
Kevin Christopher Gibson
Koré DéShawn Carpenter
Jamese Annette Lewis
Jasmyn Charlise Lewis
–for sharing me with the world, realizing that for
this cause came I forth into the world ~

Introduction

Objective

To checkmate the enemy and deny him access into our lives

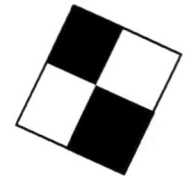

Checkmate

In chess and other board games within that family, checkmate occurs when one player's king is threatened with capture, and there is no way to meet that threat; hence, the player who is checkmated loses the game.

Without a doubt, the enemy is allowed to roam free until the appointed time, at which point his capture and fate is inevitable. Until that time, we've been given what we need to checkmate the enemy, his imps, and even his devices to render their attempts to wreak havoc in our lives null and void.

The enemy's goal is to hinder, and

TOOLS OF THE BELIEVER

prevent, if we allow him, us from completing the work Christ began and commissioned us to do. (Matthew 28:19-20)

Yet, God has given us power over all the works of the enemy (Luke 9:1) —even the power to tie his hands – to bind his devices and render them impotent in our lives.

No weapon that has been formed against the body of Christ, the body of believers, shall prosper! (Isaiah 54:17)

> We've been given what we need to checkmate the enemy, his imps, and even his devices to render their attempts to wreak havoc in our lives null and void.

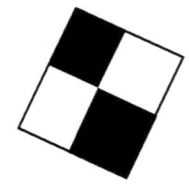

Access Denied

Submit yourselves therefore to God. Resist the devil, and he will flee from you.
~ James 4:7 ~

We have the power and authority to resist the devil. God has given us what we need in order to withstand, even to stand firm against, the enemy.

We resist the devil when we refuse to operate in deception, in doubt, in disobedience, in division, and in distraction, thereby checkmating the enemy, even denying him access into our lives through those devices.

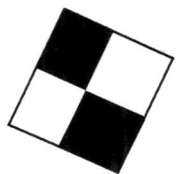

The Players...

You

...AKA a Christian, a Believer, part of the Body of Christ

...saved by grace

...a new creature in Christ

...filled with the Holy Ghost

...more than a conqueror

...a soldier of Jesus Christ

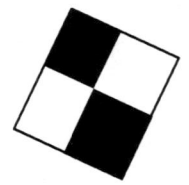

The Players...

The Opponent—
the devil and his imps

...AKA Satan, Lucifer, the enemy

...known to seek whom he may destroy

...desires to sift you as wheat

...jealous of you

...a defeated foe

...trying to take as many with him as possible

...trying to keep you from completing your assignments and from fulfilling your purpose

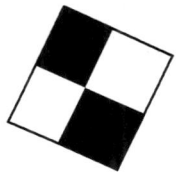

The Players...

Wheat— your brothers and sisters in Christ

...those who have accepted Jesus Christ as their personal Lord and Savior

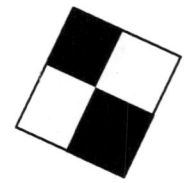

The Players...

Tares—the unsaved

...those who have not yet accepted Jesus Christ as their Lord and Savior

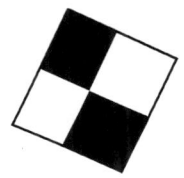

The Players...
Father, Son, Holy Ghost

...**F**aithful, **A**lpha & Omega, **T**ruth, **H**oly, **E**ternal, **R**ighteous

...**S**avior, **O**mnipotent, **N**othing is too hard for HIM

...**H**elper, **O**mniscient, **L**ORD, **Y**HWH, **G**OD, **H**ealer, **O**mnipresent, **S**hepherd, **T**riune God

The Lord our God is one Lord!
(Deuteronomy 6:4/Mark 12:29)

TOOLS OF THE BELIEVER

15

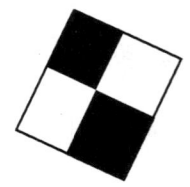

The Strategies...
Strategy #1 –
Recognize Satan's Devices

Chicanery –
Using shifts and tricks

The enemy operates by utilizing chicanery (shifts and tricks), planting tares amongst the wheat and leaving behind the resulting residue and snares of deception, doubt, disobedience, division, and distraction in the body. When we are equipped, we are able to stand against these wiles of the devil.

~ 2 Corinthians 2:11 ~
Lest Satan should get an advantage of us: for we are not ignorant of his devices.

Without a doubt, we, as believers, need not be ignorant of satan's devices, for throughout the word of God, we find that the enemy's devices, even his weaponry, have been revealed.

Behold, I have created the smith that bloweth the coals in the fire, and that bringeth forth an instrument for his work; and I have created the waster to destroy. No weapon that is formed against thee shall prosper; and every tongue that shall rise against thee in judgment thou shalt condemn. This is the heritage of the servants of the LORD, and their righteousness is of me, saith the LORD. ~ Isaiah 54:16–17 ~

Although many in the body don't want to

talk about the enemy, rather pretending that he does not exist, even ignoring, the enemy is real, and the enemy does exist because the Bible tells us so! And lest satan should get an advantage of us, we must not be ignorant of his devices! When we are equipped, we are not vulnerable or don't have to worry about falling prey to the enemy, his imps, or even his devices.

Without a doubt, we, as believers, even as Christians, have the Holy Spirit, and are assured that Greater is He that is in us than he that is in the world. (I John 4:4) Even still, all too often believers fall prey to the enemy's devices, ignorant of and oblivious to the fact that they are indeed devices of the enemy, ones that can only serve to lead us out of the will of God, ones that can hinder us from fulfilling our purpose and from completing our assignments.

If you find yourself the author or even

the victim of such, then you are falling prey to the snares of the enemy! In the body of Christ, even believers, we have persons caught up in one or more of those snares! Yet, we have the power to recognize the enemy's tricks and even deny him access into our lives!

We need to use the tools that God has given us as believers, even our weapons, *for the weapons of our warfare are not carnal, but mighty through God to the pulling down of strongholds! ~ II Corinthians 10:4 ~*

> Yet, we have the power to recognize the enemy's tricks and even deny him access into our lives!

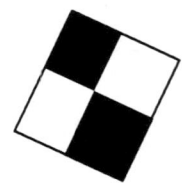

Strategy # 2 –
Use the Tools that God Has Given Us as Believers

The Bible makes it clear that we must put on the whole armour of God that we may be able to stand against the wiles of the devil. (Ephesians 6:11)

God has given us, as believers, tools that equip us to be able to stand, even to withstand, those wiles of the devil.

As believers, those wiles should not be a part of our lives, even of our character, for they are associated with the flesh, and we die daily to

TOOLS OF THE BELIEVER

the flesh. (I Corinthians 15:31) Before we became followers of Jesus Christ, we practiced and participated in deception, doubt, disobedience, division, and distraction, but now that we are out of the darkness, and we are in His marvelous light, which is where we should dwell, we are to walk in Truth, Faith, Obedience, Unity, all that we may Be About Our Father's Business.

We can stand against the wiles of the devil until that great day when wrong is made right; when every knee shall bow and every tongue shall confess; when Jesus Himself will reign supreme over the whole earth; when there will be no more crying and no more dying; when we will see the King, even King Jesus, in all of His glory! But until that time, we can Checkmate the enemy, his imps, and even his devices!

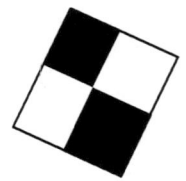

The Premise

The premise of this book is that the reader is saved. Indeed the truth is hid from the unbeliever. *But if our gospel be hid, it is hid to them that are lost . ~ II Corinthians 4:3 ~*

If you don't know Jesus Christ as Lord and Savior of your life, stop now and receive the plan of salvation. Repeat the following:

Dear Lord, forgive me for my sins. I am ready to surrender all and give my life to you. I believe that you became flesh and were born of the Virgin Mary, that you died on the cross for my sins, and that you rose again the third day with all power. According to Your Word, dear God, in *Romans 10:9*, I believe *That if thou shalt confess with thy mouth the Lord Jesus, and shalt believe in thine heart that God hath raised him from the dead, thou shalt be saved.* On this day, dear God, I thank you for saving me and becoming Lord and Savior of my life. Dear Lord, fill me today with your precious Holy Ghost.

In Jesus' name I pray, Amen.

CHECKMATE!

Device # 1: *Deception*
  CHECKMATE: **TRUTH**

Device # 2: *Doubt*
  CHECKMATE: **FAITH**

Device # 3: *Disobedience*
  CHECKMATE: **OBEDIENCE**

Device # 4: *Division*
  CHECKMATE: **UNITY**

Device # 5: *Distraction*
  CHECKMATE: **BEING ABOUT OUR FATHER'S BUSINESS**

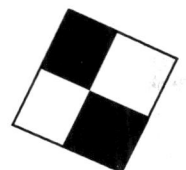

Device # 1: Deception -
Being false or untruthful; not doing what one said he or she would do

Deception is one of the primary devices of the enemy. Some have even termed him the master of deception.

And the great dragon was cast out, that old serpent, called the Devil, and Satan, which deceiveth the whole world: he was cast out into the earth, and his angels were cast out with him.

~ Revelation12:9 ~

We must not indulge in being false or untruthful or of not doing what we say we will do. We must not mislead, delude, or beguile others.

Many people operate as if deception is okay. They even attempt to excuse it or lessen the offense of it, even referring to things as "little white lies," or "stories," suggesting that there's no harm in "some" lies, even in "some" deception, becoming a willing participant of the enemy's snare of deception.

The word of God makes it clear that the devil is a liar, and the father of it. *Ye are of your father the devil, and the lusts of your father ye will do. He was a murderer from the beginning, and abode not in the truth, because there is no truth in him. When he speaketh a lie, he speaketh of his own: for he is a liar, and the father of it.*
~ John 8:44 ~

As believers, even as Christians – which means *followers* of Jesus Christ, we cannot at any point or under any circumstances convince our-

TOOLS OF THE BELIEVER

selves that it's okay to be false to, to intentionally mislead, to delude, or to beguile others.

The Word of God makes it clear that it is wrong for us to deceive others. *Be not a witness against thy neighbour without cause; and deceive not with thy lips. ~ Proverbs 24:28 ~*

As well, we must take heed lest we be deceived. *And Jesus answering them began to say, Take heed lest any man deceive you.*
~ Mark 13:5 ~ We must beware and be aware anytime we are tempted to indulge in any type of deception: fraud, double-dealing, subterfuge, trickery or cheating, for without a doubt, it is a trick, even a stratagem of the enemy!

As believers, why do we think it is okay or acceptable to practice or participate in deception? Many in the body practice deception in their marriages, on their jobs, and in various aspects of their day-to-day lives. How can we expect God to be pleased if we are being dishonest with our mates and in business practices? Is that the kind of witness we desire to have -- cheating in our marriages, stealing on our jobs, duping customers, deceiving government agencies? Yet, many in the body of Christ do just that and never stop to consider that operating in such deception hinders their walk with God.

We must return to the day of when our word was bond! In other words, what we said meant something! If we said we were going to do something, then we could be counted on to do just that!

As you examine your life, in what areas are you allowing deception and dishonesty to dwell?

Examine your relationships, your conversations with your family members and loved ones, as well as your actions and interactions on

TOOLS OF THE BELIEVER

the job. There is a danger in being the author of deception for the word says, *Be not deceived; God is not mocked: for whatsoever a man soweth, that shall he also reap. ~ Galatians 6:7 ~* Furthermore, that *evil men and seducers shall wax worse and worse, deceiving, and being deceived. ~ II Timothy 3:13 ~*

Indeed, we need not deceive ourselves into believing that it is okay to practice deceit, in any form, for it always has been and still remains a stratagem of the enemy. We can checkmate the enemy's device of deception and deny him access into our lives through that snare by refusing to operate in deception and by choosing to walk in truth!

> Checkmate the enemy by refusing to operate in deception!

CHECKMATE: WALKING IN TRUTH

Truth:

–Jesus saith unto him, I am the way, the truth, and the life: no man cometh unto the Father, but by me. ~ John 14:6 ~

– Pilate saith unto him, What is truth? And when he had said this, he went out again unto the Jews, and saith unto them, I find in him no fault at all. ~ John 18:38 ~

Why must we walk in truth?

The Word makes it clear that as children of the most high God, we are commanded to walk in truth!

I rejoiced greatly that I found of thy children walking in truth, as we have received a commandment from the Father. ~ II John 1:4 ~

I have no greater joy than to hear that my children walk in truth. ~ III John 1:4 ~

As well, we are to practice honesty at all times, speaking truth with one another.

Wherefore putting away lying, speak every man truth with his neighbour: for we are members one of another. ~ Ephesians 4:25 ~

Without a doubt, the Word of God is clear that we must walk in truth, that our heavenly Father might be pleased with us. As believers, we must know that truth is always right, and that honesty is indeed the best policy!

How do we walk in truth?

We walk in truth by practicing honesty and integrity at all times and by being reliable. That doesn't mean we speak much; on the contrary, we choose our words wisely and always give the truth, in love.

Many claim to preach the truth, but love is absent, hence causing the truth to not be well received. As well, many don't rightly divide the word, so their version of truth is faulty! We can remedy this by studying to shew ourselves approved unto God, workmen that needeth not to be ashamed rightly dividing the word of truth (II Timothy 2:15) and by seeking the Holy Spirit for interpretation of the scriptures.

Let us choose to walk in truth and practice honesty at all times. Indeed, the truth shall make us free—even free from the bondage of sin!

TOOLS OF THE BELIEVER

As Christians, we should strive to walk in truth, that there may be no fault in us.

> Let us choose to walk in truth and practice honesty at all times.

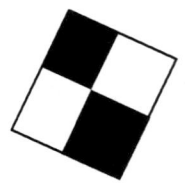

Device # 2: Doubt -
Unconfident, untrusting, unsure, uncertain, unbelief

Doubt is another one of the enemy's primary devices. When we operate in doubt, then we experience defeat in many areas and aspects of our lives.

Doubt is associated with fear, and we know that God hath not given us the spirit of fear, but of power, and of love, and of a sound mind. (II Timothy 1:7)

Many times, we won't even try, because of doubt. We give up even before we start. We are defeated at the beginning, because of our doubt.

By operating in doubt, we are hindered from doing the things God has instructed us to do. If we doubt the power of prayer, we won't pray. If we doubt the importance of fasting, then we won't fast. If we doubt the necessity of tithing, then we won't tithe. If we doubt the need to honor God with our praise and thanksgiving, then we won't have God as the center of our lives. If we doubt the importance of reading and studying the Word of God for ourselves, then we won't spend time in the Word. If we doubt that ALL things work together for our good, and that God is in control, then we won't totally trust God. If we doubt the need to seek first the kingdom of God and His righteousness, then we'll find ourselves seeking after other things.

Indeed, the enemy's snare of doubt can be extremely destructive in the lives of Christians. When we don't do those things God has instructed us to do, we don't experience the abundant life that God desires for us to have. The Word of God tells us *The thief cometh not, but for to steal, and to kill, and to destroy: I am come that they might have life, and that they might have it more abundantly! ~ John 10:10 ~*

Doubt can serve to cancel out the promises and blessings of God for our lives. Regardless of the situation or circumstance, we must not succumb to doubt.

Doubt prevents us from stepping out and doing those things God has told us to do! Because many are operating in doubt, coupled with fear, they are not completing their God-given assignments nor fulfilling their God-given purpose in life.

As you examine your life, what things has God told you to do, even through His Spirit, that you have not done as a result of doubt and

TOOLS OF THE BELIEVER

fear?

We can checkmate the enemy's device of doubt and deny him access into our lives through that snare by refusing to operate in doubt and by choosing to walk by faith!

> Checkmate the enemy by refusing to operate in doubt!

CHECKMATE: WALKING BY FAITH

Faith:

— Now faith is the substance of things hoped for, the evidence of things not seen. ~ Hebrews 11:1 ~

— But without faith it is impossible to please him: for he that cometh to God must believe that he is, and that he is a rewarder of them that diligently seek him ~ Hebrews 11:6 ~

Why must we walk by faith?

Throughout the Word, *by our faith* is reiterated. The woman with the issue of blood was healed *by her faith*. (Matthew 9:20-21) The dumb were able to speak *by faith* and the blind were able to see *by faith*. (Matthew 15:31)

Indeed, in order to do those things God has called and assigned us to do, we must have faith! It is a faith walk! We can't go by how things look or appear. If God said it, we must have faith and walk it out!

How do we walk by faith?

We walk by faith by believing the impossible. *If thou canst believe, all things are possible to him that believeth. ~ Mark 9:23 ~* We must believe the impossible, and we must see the invisible. Faith means I may not be able to see it with my physical eye, but it is visible with my spiritual

eye! We must walk by faith and not by sight.
(II Corinthians 5:7)

Faith means I just believe it! If God said it, it shall come to pass! According to the word, namely *Habakkuk 2:4 and Romans 1:17*, it says *The just shall live by faith.*

Faith—in other words our belief—is essential! With Faith, it doesn't matter how it seems! It doesn't matter what man has to say, for God always has the last word! And as Jeremiah said in his prayer in *Jeremiah 32:17 Ah Lord God! Behold, thou hast made the heaven and the earth by thy great power and stretched out arm, and there is nothing too hard for thee!*

Matthew 19:26 adds *But Jesus beheld them, and said unto them, With men this is impossible; but with God all things are possible.*

We walk by faith by totally trusting God. We accomplish this by leaning not unto our own understanding, but in all our ways acknowledging

TOOLS OF THE BELIEVER

Him, that He may direct our paths.
(Proverbs 3:5-6)

Also, we accomplish this by knowing that all things work together for good to them that love God, to them who are the called according to His purpose. (Romans 8:28)

Let us choose to walk by faith regardless of the situation or circumstance, having our confidence in Him.

As Christians, we should strive to walk by faith, that God may be pleased.

Let us choose to walk by faith regardless of the situation or circumstance, having our confidence in Him!

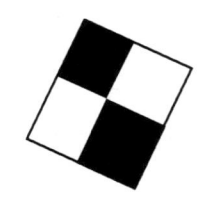

Device # 3: Disobedience - *Refusing to obey*

Disobedience is another device of the enemy. He wants us to operate in disobedience. He does not want us to obey God!

As the enemy refused to submit to God's authority, hence, disobeying God, he wants us to be disobedient and to refuse to submit to authority, even to refuse to obey.

Submission is practically a dirty word these days. Submit involves yielding or surrendering oneself to the authority or will of another. Many people struggle with submitting. They are not willing to yield to authority; they are not willing to surrender their wills for that of another.

As a result, many refuse to submit to anybody or to anything. Husbands don't want to submit to Jesus Christ. Wives don't want to submit to their husbands. Children don't want to submit to their parents. Church members don't want to submit to their Pastors or the Pastor's vision. As well, many refuse to obey, not wanting to obey them that have rule over them. Many don't want to obey the laws of the land or even God's laws. Many simply do not want to submit to or obey authority!

How can we think it is okay to not submit, to not obey? Even Jesus submitted! Even Jesus obeyed! *And he went a little farther, and fell on his face, and prayed , saying, O my Father, if it be possible, let this cup pass from me: nevertheless not as I will, but as thou wilt.*
~ Matthew 26:39 ~

We must not allow the enemy to rob us

of the blessings as a result of disobedience. The word is clear regarding the rewards of obedience as well as the consequences of disobedience. (Deuteronomy 28)

Many in the body are experiencing many of the consequences of disobedience. They refuse to walk in obedience, and as a result experience the consequences wherever they go and in whatever they do.

Many are disobedient to the things of God by walking according to the course of this world, fulfilling the lusts of their flesh and the desires of their flesh and mind!

Wherein in time past ye walked according to the course of this world, according to the prince of the power of the air, the spirit that now worketh in the children of disobedience: Among whom also we all had our conversation in times past in the lusts of our flesh, fulfilling the desires

of the flesh and of the mind; and were by nature the children of wrath, even as others.
~ Ephesians 2:2-3 ~

Many are disobedient and allowing the flesh to rule, walking in carnality. It's about them and what they want! It's not about God's will, God's way, or God's word. They want to do what they want to do! Their wills supersede God's will for their lives; their ways outweigh God's way; and their many words take precedence over God's word! Many of our walks are hindered because we are operating in disobedience! As you examine your life, are there any areas of disobedience in your life?

We can checkmate the enemy's device of disobedience and deny him access into our lives through that snare by refusing to operate in disobedience and by choosing to walk in obedience!

Checkmate the enemy by refusing to operate in disobedience!

CHECKMATE:
WALKING IN OBEDIENCE

Obedience:

— Ye shall walk after the LORD your God, and fear him, and keep his commandments, and obey his voice, and ye shall serve him, and cleave unto him.

~ Deuteronomy 13:4 ~

— Thou shalt therefore obey the voice of the LORD thy God, and do his commandments and his statutes, which I command thee this day.

~ Deuteronomy 27:10 ~

Why must we walk in obedience?

We are commanded to obey God, even to keep His commandments. Jesus said that those who obey God, even whosoever shall do the will of God, the same is His brother, and sister, and mother. (Mark 3:35) As children of the most high God, we ought to obey our heavenly father, just as children are to obey their earthly parents. As believers, if we are going to walk with God, then we must walk in obedience!

Indeed, we will even be rewarded as a result of walking in obedience. If we be willing and obedient, we will eat the good of the land. (Isaiah 1:19) Many desire to eat the good of the land; however, they are not willing nor are they obedient to the things of God.

Deuteronomy 28 provides some of the rewards of obedience.

¹And it shall come to pass, if thou shalt hearken diligently unto the voice of the LORD thy God, to observe and to do all his commandments which I command thee this day, that the LORD thy God will set thee on high above all nations of the earth:

²And all these blessings shall come on thee, and overtake thee, if thou shalt hearken unto the voice of the LORD thy God.

³Blessed shalt thou be in the city, and blessed shalt thou be in the field.

⁴Blessed shall be the fruit of thy body, and the fruit of thy ground, and the fruit of thy cattle, the increase of thy kine, and the flocks of thy sheep.

⁵Blessed shall be thy basket and thy store.

⁶Blessed shalt thou be when thou comest in, and blessed shalt thou be when thou goest out.

We must learn to obey God, no matter what! I

know it's hard sometimes, even that the Spirit is willing but the flesh is weak, but we must learn to bring this flesh under subjection. We must lay aside every weight, and the sin which doth so easily beset us! (Hebrews 12:1) We must say, Nevertheless, not my will, but thine will be done! As Jesus submitted and obeyed the Father, so must we!

How do we walk in obedience?
We walk in obedience by mortifying the flesh.

Colossians 3:5-7
⁵Mortify therefore your members which are upon the earth; fornication, uncleanness, inordinate affection, evil concupiscence, and covetousness, which is idolatry:

⁶For which things' sake the wrath of God cometh on the children of disobedience:

⁷In the which ye also walked some time, when ye lived in them.

We cannot allow the flesh to rule, walking in carnality. It must not be about us and what we want! When we pursue the things of the Spirit (whatsoever things are true and honest and just and pure and lovely and of good report – Philippians 4:8), instead of the things of the flesh, we walk in obedience.

We walk in obedience by living according to God's word, God's will, and God's way.

We must not only believe but obey, hence live, by every word that proceedeth out of the mouth of God. (Matthew 4:4) God's word is the only thing that will remain (Luke 21:33); God's will should supersede our wills (Luke 22:42); God's way is the best way (Proverbs 16:25).

Let us choose to walk in obedience, for the whole duty of man is to fear God and keep His commandments.

As Christians, we should strive to walk in obedience, even to walk after the LORD our God, and fear him, and keep his commandments, and obey his voice.

> Let us choose to walk in obedience, for the whole duty of man is to fear God and keep His commandments.

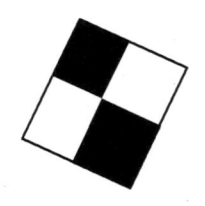

Device # 4: Division - *Separating or keeping apart*

Division is another device of the enemy. The enemy utilizes division in our homes, in the church, and even in the body of Christ to divide and conquer, all in order to hinder the work of the church, even to win souls and to make disciples, even to build up the kingdom of God! The enemy knows how effective division is; he is a master at it, even as one-third of the angels fell with him. (Revelation 12:9)

Division serves to separate and to keep us apart. When we focus on our differences, division results, as opposed to the complements and appreciation of diversity that should result.

For many in the body of Christ, division is evident in our homes, in our churches, and even in the body of Christ as a whole.

    We see division in our homes, even in our marriages, even though the Word makes it clear that the two (husband and wife) shall be one flesh! (Genesis 2:22-24), in other words, be unified, a single unit, walking in agreement. Yet, we see division in many Christian marriages: This is my money, and that is your money! This is my car, and that is your car! With blended families, these are my children, and those are your children! If you've managed to obtain some things before marrying, these are my things, and those are your things. Saints, that's operating in division. That's not being one! When husband and wife are not one, their prayers will be hindered (I Peter 3:7) and the disharmony will flow down to the kids. A house divided against itself cannot stand. (Mark 3:25)

As well, we see division in the church. As long as there is church member against church member and minister against minister, the work of the Lord is hindered, even in that church. In many churches, we are competing and not completing! We lose focus and begin to compete and not to complete! We begin to feel that our gifts, our abilities, even what we bring to the table is unimportant and insignificant by comparing it to another's gift.

Furthermore, we see division in the body of Christ, all intended to separate and divide us, all to hinder the work of Christ being done, even the work of the kingdom, for there's only one body and one kingdom that believers should be trying to build, and that's the kingdom of God!

Yet, some only fellowship and worship with those of like denomination! The Word makes it clear there's one body! (Ephesians 4:4)

Indeed, the word says, "Can two walk together, except they be agreed?" (Amos 3:3) Don't we agree that Jesus Christ is the way, the truth, and the life - that no man cometh unto the Father but by Him? (John 14:6) That Jesus Christ is come in the flesh? (I John 4:2) Don't we agree that the Bible is the Word of God? (II Timothy 3:16) Are we Christians = followers of Jesus Christ? Are we believers? Do we live by every word that proceedeth out of the mouth of God? (Matthew 4:4) Then we can walk together, for we are one body!

We know that the enemy does not want us to be one body; he does not want us to complete the work that Christ began. He wants us to be divided, and he does whatever he can to create division. He uses a number of tricks, devices and snares to accomplish this.

As you examine your life, in what areas are you allowing division to operate?

We can checkmate the enemy's device of division and deny him access into our lives through that snare by refusing to operate in division and by choosing to walk in unity in our homes, in our churches, and even in the body of Christ!

Checkmate the enemy by refusing to operate in division!

CHECKMATE:
WALKING IN UNITY

Unity:

– Behold, how good and how pleasant it is for brethren to dwell together in unity!

~ Psalm 133:1 ~

Why must we walk in unity?

As the body of Christ, we should walk in unity. According to the Word of God, we are one body. *There is one body, and one Spirit, even as ye are called in one hope of your calling; One Lord, one faith, one baptism, One God and Father of all, who is above all, and through all, and in you all.*
~ Ephesians 4:4-6 ~

As one body, we have a common goal: *And he gave some, apostles; and some, prophets; and some, evangelists; and some, pastors and teachers; For the perfecting of the saints, for the work of the ministry, for the edifying of the body of Christ: Till we all come in the unity of the faith, and of the knowledge of the Son of God, unto a perfect man, unto the measure of the stature of the fulness of Christ: That we henceforth be no more children, tossed to and fro, and carried about with every wind of doctrine, by the sleight of men, and cunning craftiness, whereby they lie in wait to deceive; But speaking the truth in love, may grow up into him in all things, which is the head, even Christ: From whom the whole body fitly joined together and compacted by that which every joint supplieth, according to the effectual working in the measure of every part, maketh increase of the body unto the edifying of itself in love. ~ Ephesians 4:11-16 ~*

Everybody is needed! Everybody has a part to play; no matter how seemingly small, it is important! Consider the function of a fingernail or a toenail. Can you imagine how painful it would be if one were removed? A little thing, but it is needed! It is still important! It still has a function, even a purpose!

In other words, although we have different gifts, all gifts are important, useful, and needful! They all work together. One body, many members, each doing his part, as unto the Lord, accountable to God!

How do we walk in unity?

We walk in unity by coming together as husbands and wives; by coming together as church families; by coming together as the body of Christ. When we know who we are, and whose we are, we are able to come together, appreciating our differences, and allowing our gifts to work together for the up building of the kingdom of God. We walk in unity by understanding our roles, even our parts. When we understand what the word of God says about our roles as wives and as husbands, we are able to walk in unity in our marriages. When we understand what the word of God says about our callings, and giftings and how they are to be used, working together, for the up building of God's kingdom, we are able to walk in unity. When we understand what God's word says about other believers, about what constitutes a Christian, about what constitutes salvation, about being one body, we are able to walk in unity as the body of Christ. We must spend time in the word, reading, studying, and meditating on it; furthermore, we must allow the Holy Spirit to give us the understanding of the scriptures. When we submit to God's word and to the Holy Spirit, we are able to walk in unity.

Let us choose to walk in unity and come together as husbands and wives, as churches, and as the body of Christ!

As Christians, we should strive to walk in unity, for we are one body!

> **Let us choose to walk in unity and come together as husbands and wives, as churches, and as the body of Christ!**

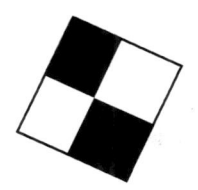

Device # 5: Distraction –
Unfocused or off-task as a result of worry or trouble

Another device of the enemy is that of distraction! When we are distracted, we are rendered impotent, inefficient and ineffective.

Have you ever been pulled in different directions, even stirred up or confused when it came to doing those things God would have you to do? Have you ever been so disturbed, troubled, upset, or vexed that you couldn't do those things God had for you to do?

The enemy desires to divert us from the things of God, even to sidetrack us and draw us away or lead us astray.

The enemy uses four primary modes of distraction: being too busy; being outside of our assignments; being consumed with the cares of this world; being entertained.

Some are distracted because they are too busy, even consumed with so many things, trying to do too much, too many things, things we are not even called to do, hence being a jack of all trades and a master of none. In essence, we are out of order, doing things that we think may be good to do but not necessarily what we should be doing. Consider the story of Mary and Martha. (Luke 10: 38-42)

Others are distracted because they are outside of their assignments. How can we expect to hear God say Well done, even when we're not doing what He told us to do? While we're doing things we're not called to do, those things we are called to do are neglected, even going undone, and indeed God raises up another to do them. When we are distracted and outside of our assignments, we are hindered from doing what God has placed us here to do, even from fulfilling our purposes in life and from completing our assignments. Since many in the body don't know what it is they've been called to do, they end up doing any and everything, all in the name of service to the Lord.

Another mode of distraction that plagues many in the body is being consumed with the cares of this world. Many times the enemy will bring things into our lives that serve to distract us from God; he wants us to focus on our problems, instead of focusing on the problem-solver! He wants us pulled in different directions, confused emotionally, instead of looking unto Jesus the author and finisher of our faith. (Hebrews 12:2) He wants us to worry and be troubled, but we must realize that they are merely distractions, designed to get us off track and off course!

Another way of diverting us from the things of God is through entertainment. In many places of worship, the focus is on being entertained as opposed to being equipped! In order for the body to be equipped, the focus must be on the Word, even on Jesus, the living Word! The primary focus cannot be on the praise singers or the praise dancers but on He who is worthy of all praise! The primary focus can't be on the gifts but on He who is the giver of gifts. It is time out for the body to be entertained! It's time that we, as a body, are equipped!

As you examine your life, are you distracted from God's will for your life as a result of being too busy, being outside your assignment, being consumed with the cares of this world, or of being entertained?

We must bind the enemy's device of distraction, and not allow him to cause us to be distracted, off task, unfocused, even ignorant to what it is that God has called us to do and of what God would have us to do!

We can checkmate the enemy's device of distraction and deny him access into our lives through that snare by refusing to operate in distraction and by choosing to be about our Father's business!

> **Checkmate the enemy by refusing to operate in distraction!**

CHECKMATE: BEING ABOUT OUR FATHER'S BUSINESS

Being About Our Father's Business:

- And he said unto them, How is it that ye sought me? wist ye not that I must be about my Father's business? ~ Luke 2:49 ~

How do we ensure that we are being about our Father's business?

We can be about our Father's business by focusing on those things that God has called us to do, by ensuring that we are in alignment for our assignments, by not being consumed with the cares of this world, and by seeking to be equipped.

We should seek God regarding our purpose and our assignments. If we are misplaced, we should get in alignment for our assignments. The arm cannot effectively do what the leg was designed to do; the eye cannot do what the ear was designed to do!

As well, we can ensure that we are not consumed with the cares of this world by casting all of our care upon Him, for he careth for us. (I Peter 5:7)

Finally, we must seek to be equipped by being a part of a Christ-centered body of believers, not forsaking the assembling of ourselves together, as the manner of some is; but exhorting one another: and so much the more, as ye see the day approaching. (Hebrews 10:25) We must desire the sincere milk of the word, that we may grow thereby. (I Peter 2:2) When we are focused, on track, and in alignment for our assignments, we can be effective for the kingdom of God!

As Christians, let us choose to be about our Father's business, that we may hear him say, *Well done, good and faithful servant; thou hast been faithful over a few things, I will make thee ruler over many things: enter thou into the joy of the Lord!* ~ *Matthew 25:23* ~

> **As Christians, let us choose to be about our Father's business, that we may hear him say, Well done!**

In Conclusion...
It's a Choice!

We can choose to operate in deception, doubt, disobedience, division, and distraction, *or* we can choose to walk in truth, in faith, in obedience, in unity and be about our Father's business. The word says *And if it seem evil unto you to serve the LORD, choose you this day whom ye will serve.* ~ *Joshua 24:15* ~ The choice is ours. Which will you choose?

Afterword

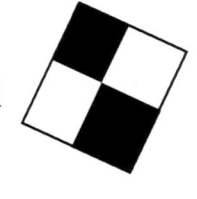

Book 3
Tools of the Believer—Exposed: Your Witness Is on Display

All too often, many in the body of Christ fall prey to additional devices, even wiles of the devil, namely Hate, Sorrow, Unrest, Impatience, Harshness, Wickedness, Unbelief, Brashness, and Excess.

Many believers find themselves in trouble as they choose to involve themselves in those devices; however, without a doubt, we can put those works of the enemy, even of the flesh, in check, by choosing to walk in the fruit of the Spirit, namely Love, Joy, Peace, Longsuffering, Gentleness, Goodness, Faith, Meekness, and Temperance. (Galatians 5:22–24)

TOOLS OF THE BELIEVER

CHECKMATE: ACCESS DENIED!

Checkmate: Access Denied! is book 2 in the ten-book series. In chess and other board games within that family, checkmate occurs when one player's king is threatened with capture and there is no way to meet that threat; hence, the player who is checkmated loses the game. Without a doubt, the enemy is allowed to roam free until the appointed time, at which point his capture and fate is inevitable. Until that time, we've been given what we need to checkmate the enemy, his imps, and even his devices to render their attempts to wreak havoc in our lives null and void...

TOOLS OF THE BELIEVER is committed to assisting in the equipping of God's people, that they might be able to stand against the wiles of the devil, for the weapons of our warfare are not carnal, but mighty through God to the pulling down of strongholds!

CHERYL JEFFRIES is a minister of the Gospel of Jesus Christ. Her calling is to assist in tearing Satan's kingdom down through preaching, teaching, and writing for the purpose of equipping God's people.

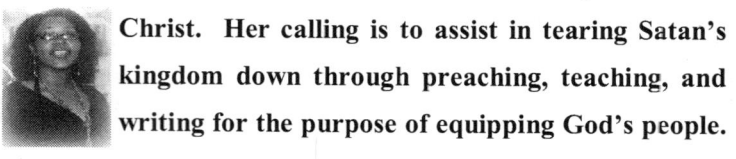